Machine

M000119837

A Comprehensive Journey From Beginner To Advanced Level To Understand WHY You MUST Keep Pace With Innovation, Artificial Intelligence And Big Data With Practical Examples

JOSEPH MINING

Additionally, the information in the following pages is intended only for informational purposes and should thus be thought of as universal. As befitting its nature, it is presented without assurance regarding its prolonged validity or interim quality. Trademarks that are mentioned are done without written consent and can in no way be considered an endorsement from the trademark holder.

Table of Contents

Introduction

The following chapters will discuss everything that you need to know in order to get started with machine learning. The world of technology is growing at a fast pace. There seem to be new things coming out on the market all the time, and the consumer is ready to welcome it in and enjoy every minute of the whole thing. But due to this increase in demand, programmers need to find newer and better ways to impress the customer and machine learning is helping them to do just that.

While there are a lot of different components that come with machine learning, it is important to realize that this is basically a way of coding that allows the computer or the other pieces of technology to learn as it goes. The user is able to put in any kind of input that they would like (without the programmer trying to figure it all out ahead of time and make guesses) and the computer will use past experiences and other information to help out and learn over time. it is a really neat thing that has shaped a lot of the technology industry including with spam filtering, search engines, voice recognition, and more.

This guidebook is going to take some time to talk more about machine learning and all of the different parts that come with it. Inside, we will start out with some of the basics of machine learning. We will look at what machine learning is, why it is so beneficial to learn, and even how it compares to artificial intelligence and more.

From there, we are going to take a look at how statistics and probability can be added into this mix in order to help make machine learning more effective overall and some of the building blocks that are needed to help with machine learning. Through all of this, we will look at examples and formulas that help to bring this alive and ensures that you are going to understand how these affect machine learning fully.

To end this guidebook, we are going to take a look at some of the basic algorithms that are found with machine learning. These include the three basic types of machine learning, including supervised learning, unsupervised learning, and reinforcement learning. Inside each, we will talk about the algorithms, the strengths, and weaknesses of each, and when you would benefit from using them all.

Machine learning is changing the way that technology works, and there are a ton of different opportunities that come with it. There are just so many possibilities that are now available to us thanks to machine learning that just weren't possible with some of the traditional coding methods that we have used in the past. When you are ready to learn more about how machine learning works and how you can utilize it on some of your own projects, make sure to check out this guidebook to help you get started!

There are plenty of books on this subject on the market, thanks again for choosing this one! Every effort was made to ensure it is full of as much useful information as possible; please enjoy!

Chapter 1: What is Machine Learning?

If you have spent any time looking up information about technology and where our world is going now in terms of using computers and programming, then it is likely that you have spent at least a little time hearing about machine learning. Whether you were intrigued by this term or only saw it pop up on some of the articles you were reading, you will find that machine learning is actually a very important thing to know how to work with. It can really open the doors to new types of programming that you are able to do, and can make life easier when it comes to developing the software and technology that you want.

If you are new to this arena and haven't spent much time with programming, then it is possible that you have never even heard about machine learning. Even so, it is likely that at one point or another, you have actually used machine learning to help make your life easier. For example, if you have ever done a query on a search engine, such as on Google, then it was the technology of machine learning that made this possible. The program that runs these search engine sites and helps you to find the results that you want are powered by machine learning.

Machine learning technology is the only way that you will be able to get these kinds of programs to work. Regular coding is not able to do this complex of a task. The system needs to be able to read through your request, look through millions of websites, and then pick out the one that matches up to your needs. And in the beginning, it may not do the best job picking out what you want. But thanks to the machine learning technology behind it, these programs are able to learn your search preferences and will learn exactly what you are looking for, based on the options that you choose.

That is just one of the many examples that can come with how we will use machine learning to do some really neat things. Not only can the use of search engines benefit from this technology, but you can use it in many other applications, such as trying to figure out whether a message should be considered spam or not.

Unlike some of the conventional programming methods that you may have used in the past, machine learning can help programs to not just sit still and give out predetermined outputs. This works in some cases, but it is not going to be efficient for a lot of the things we want to do. Unlike these conventional programs, machine learning programs are designed in order to learn and adapt based on the behavior that the user portrays to it. This is a great thing because it ensures that the user is going to get the results that they want, rather than being frustrated along the way.

If a computer or another form of technology already has some machine learning capabilities or programs on it, can be programmed in a way to form the inputs that the user gives to it. This means that the computer is able to provide the user with the results, or the answers, that are needed, even if the problem is more complex. The input for this kind of learning process, which is often known as a learning algorithm, will be known as data training in this kind of process.

Understanding machine learning

When we are talking about machine learning, it is basically the process of teaching the program or the computer to use some of its own experiences that happen over time, the experiences with the user, in order to do a better job of providing results in the future.

A good example of this would be a program that is used in order to filter out the spam emails that you get. There are a few different methods out there that you can use to make this happen. But one of the easiest ones that you can use here is to teach the computer how you would like it to identify, memorize, and categorize all of the emails that are in your inbox by labeling them as either safe or spam when they first enter into your email.

As you do this over time, the computer will learn which emails you think are spam, and which ones are more important to you. Then, if there is a new email that does come in at a later tie, the program is going to take a look at how you treated similar emails in the past and will take care of them in this matter. Over time, the program is going to get really good at marking the right emails spam and leaving the others alone, but there is often a few trial and errors that happen along the way.

While this is a good technique of memorization to work with when you want to teach the program how to do these processes, there are going to be some things that are going to fall short with it. First, this method is going to miss out on a little thing known as inductive reasoning. This is something that has to be there, even with a program using machine learning, so that the computer can learn efficiently.

As the programmer, you may find that it is better for you to go through and do some programming on the computer, this way you can teach it how to discern the message types (or do the other tasks that you want with this process), rather than trying to ask the computer to go through the process and the effort it takes to memorize all of that information.

To make sure that this is a process that is as simple as possible, you would need to do some programming of the computer. This programming would involve the computer scanning any email that is in your spam folder, or anything that it already knows is spam. From this scan, the program is able to recognize some of the keywords and phrases that tend to show up in these kinds of messages.

With this information in place, the computer is able to scan through any of the new emails that try to get into your inbox. And if there is one that matches up with a lot of these key phrases and words, then they are going to be sent to the spam folder, without you even knowing.

This method may sound like it takes a lot more time to accomplish than some of the others, and you may wonder why you would want to work with this method compared to doing the other one. But it is one of the best, though there are a few things to watch. You have to be actively involved in this kind of machine learning and have the realization that sometimes the program is going to do things in the wrong way, or some messages that are spam will get through to your inbox, and some that aren't spam will end up in your spam folder.

While a person would be able to read through these emails and see the issue right away, the computer is learning as it goes. And it is much faster at doing this process. It can look through hundreds of emails in a few seconds and usually gets them sorted in the right manner. But when it comes to humans, this would not happen. You would have more accuracy, but your speed would be quite a bit lower.

So basically, machine learning is going to be the process where you will teach the computer how to learn. The program will be able to use some of the information that it already has, along with the past interactions with the user that it has and can then learn the appropriate response to help it react in the manner that you would like. There are a lot of different applications that can use this, including search engines, voice recognition, and spam email filtering. And as the world of technology grows and changes, even more, it is likely that more and more applications of this kind of technology will end up coming out as well.

What are the benefits of working with machine learning?

At this point, you may be wondering why you would want to learn how to work with machine learning. There are many different things that machine learning can help you with, but there are two main ones that we are going to focus on right now. The first one includes that using machine learning means that you are going to be able to handle any task that is too complex for the programmer to place into the computer. The second is going to include that machine learning can help with adaptively generated tasks that need to be done.

With that in mind, let's look at a few situations and why you would have to use machines to ensure that they are going to work with your program.

Complicated tasks

One way that you can use machine learning is to help with some programming tasks that are complicated. There will be some tasks that you can work on in programming that may not respond that well to conventional programming. These tasks may not have the right amount of clarity that you need to use a conventional program or they just have too much complexity with them.

The first set would be tasks that people and animals can perform. Think about speech recognition, image recognition, and driving as examples of these. Humans can do these, but if you used conventional programming tools to teach the computer how to do this, it is going to run into trouble. it is much better for the computer to learn the right way to do these tasks by receiving good outputs when they are right. Machine learning can help make this happen.

The second issue is that machine learning is able to help with tasks that are too hard for humans to do. These would include things such as going through a complex analysis where there is too much data for one person to go through well. Companies may decide to use machine learning when they wish to go through a ton of data and make decisions and predictions.

In addition, machine learning can be used in a similar manner to help with genomic data, search engines, and weather prediction. There is going to be some valuable information in all of the data sets, but humans may not have the energy or the time to go through this information, at least not in a timely manner so they will use machine learning to do it for them.

While traditional forms of programming can do a lot of neat things and have worked for years to help programmers get things done, there are some tasks that just don't work that well with these. Machine learning is able to fill in the gaps and get you the results that you are looking for.

Adaptively generated tasks

If you have worked with programming in the past, it is likely that you were able to get these programs to do a lot of really neat things along the way. Even though these can do a lot of great things that can help you to really grow your knowledge of machine learning, there are some limitations to what that kind of programming can do.

One of these limitations is that the programming methods are going to be rigid. What this means is that once you are done writing out the code, and you turn it on to implement it, the codes will always be the same. These codes are going to do the same things over and over again, that is, unless you specifically go in and change up some of the code. But these codes will never be able to learn and adapt on their own.

There will be some times when you would like to create a new program and you want it to be able to act out in different manners, or you will want it to give a reaction that goes with the input it is receiving. This is something that a conventional programming language is not going to be able to do. This is where machine learning is going to come in because it allows you to write out codes so that the program can learn and make changes.

Machine learning is easy to work with

We are going to talk about a few different algorithms and tasks that work with machine learning in a bit. And as you look through these, they will seem like they are a bit complicated. But they are actually pretty simple, and it shows you all of the cool things that you are able to do when you utilize machine learning. Many of these tasks are going to be useful, but they are too complicated to do with conventional programming methods. This would include things like facial recognition and speech recognition. While traditional forms of programming would have trouble with these, machine learning can handle them with ease.

Machine learning is a great thing to learn how to use because you are able to teach a program and a type of technology how to learn as it goes along. A good example of this is speech recognition. This type of thing is going to use machine learning to figure out what you are saying and what you need. In the beginning, the program is going to struggle a bit, trying to learn your accent and the words you like to use. For the first little bit, it is possible that you will need to repeat words and phrases in order to help the program understand what you are saying to it.

Over time though, as you use the program, the speech recognition is going to get much better at the job that it is doing, and it will get the answer right the first time. The program will learn your speech patterns, your accent, and some of the other things that it needs to get the answer right. Sometimes, if you use the program long enough and often enough, it is going to become good at making predictions for you and can provide you with the answers to these predictions as well.

If machine learning is put to use in the proper manner, it is able to do this kind of learning process, regardless of the device that it is on. This means that it will learn to listen to the way that each person speaks who is on that device. This is something that is hard to do with traditional programming options that you may have used in the past, and even if you could do it with these, the code would be really complex. But, as you will see as we progress through this guidebook, you will be able to use some simple machine learning codes in order to get similar results in no time.

While you are able to bring out machine learning to complete a number of complex actions, it is sometimes easier to use the codes that come with machine learning than you would assume. If you have ever been able to code and use programming languages of any kind in the past, you will find that working with machine learning doesn't have to be as complicated as it seems, and you will already have the basics down from this past knowledge.

Another thing that you will like about machine learning is that there are a few different options that you can use, depending on the type of program you would like to work with. The three main types, which we are going to explore a bit more as this guidebook progresses, are going to include unsupervised learning, reinforcement learning, and supervised learning. When you start to use the different methods that are provided in this guidebook to handle these types of learning, it becomes so much easier for you to get the code and the program to react the way that you would like.

As you can see, there are a lot of different benefits that come with machine learning, and you will be able to use them all to help you do a lot of cool programming tasks. We will be able to see some of the different applications of machine learning as we enter into the later part of this book, but you will notice that this really opens up a lot of doors to you in terms of what you can do with coding and programming.

How can I use machine learning?

As you start looking at machine learning, you may notice that it has changed a lot over the years and the different things that programmers are now able to do with it are pretty unique and fun. There are many established firms, as well as startups, that are using machine learning because it has done some amazing things to help their business grow. While there are a lot of applications that machine learning can help you out with, some of the methods that are the best to use, include:

- Statistical research: machine learning is a big part of IT now. You will find that machine learning will help you to go through a lot of complexity when looking through large data patterns. Some of the options that will use statistical research include search engines, credit cards, and filtering spam messages.

- Big data analysis: many companies need to be able to get through a lot of data in a short amount of time. They use this data to recognize how their customers spend money and even to make decisions and predictions about the future. This used to take a long time to have someone sit through and look at the data, but now, machine learning can do the process faster and much more efficiently. Options like election campaigns, medical fields, and retail stores have used machine learning for this purpose.

- Finances: some finance companies have also used machine learning. Stock trading online has seen a rise in the use of machine learning to help make efficient and safe decisions, and so much more.

As mentioned, these are only a few of the ways that you could use machine learning to help your business. As you add it into your business and add some IT to it, you will find that even more options are going to become available.

Are there different things machine learning can help with?

When you first hear about machine learning, you may assume that you are going to run into trouble finding ways to use this kind of technology and coding to see the results that you want. You may think that there are only a few ways that this works and that the average programmer would not be able to utilize these techniques and see the results that they would like.

The neat thing about machine learning though is that there are a lot of ways that machine learning can help make your codes better, and you may be surprised at how many different applications are able to use machine learning. There are always programmers and companies who are looking at machine learning in more depth to figure out what else they are able to do with it. With that said, some of the different challenges that machine learning is good at helping out with include

Search engines

A good example that we have brought up a bit before when it comes to machine learning is the idea that it can help out with search engines. A search engine is going to take the input from the user, mainly their search query, and they will learn from the results that you push on from the list they provide. The first few times that you start to use the search engine, you will find that you may have to go down the page a bit to find the result that you think is the most relevant.

But, as your search engine starts to learn more about the way that you look things up and what you like in terms of results, it is going to get better. Over time, as you continue to do a lot more searches over and over again, you will find that your selections will get closer to the top of the page. This is because the search engine, using machine learning, was able to get better at guessing the results that you are the most interested in.

Collaborative filtering

This is a challenge that a lot of online retailers can run into because they will use it to help them get more profits through sales. Think about when you are on a site like Amazon.com. After you do a few searches, you will then get recommendations for other products that you may want to try out. Amazon.com uses machine learning in order to figure out what items you would actually be interested in, in the hopes of helping you to make another purchase.

Doing translations

There are many times when we will want to take the words that we have, and change them to another language. Whether we are taking our native language and translating over to a different language, or taking a different language and translating back to our native language, a good translation tool can make a world of difference.

If you are working with some kind of program that is responsible for translating different things, this means that you are directly working with machine learning. The program at hand is trying to look through a document or some words and then it is trying to recognize and understand the words that are there. It isn't just about the words themselves on this though. It is also about the context of the words, the syntax, and grammar. And then, if the original document has some mistakes in it, the program is going to have an even harder time learning as it goes.

This process of machine learning can be complex because it needs to teach the program how to take one language and translate it over to another one. And many times, these translation services need to be able to do this with more than one type of language. For example, there isn't really a program that just goes from English to French. It would go from English to French or Chinese, or German, or Spanish and back again. And then it may be able to do other combinations, such as German to French or Spanish to Chinese. This adds to the level of complication.

Name identity recognition

This type of programming is where the computer will need to be able to look at names and such and figure out the entities of them. It needs to be able to look at the places, actions, names, and titles out of any document that it comes across. This can be used in a situation where you have a program that needs to digest and then also comprehend a document that you submit to it.

Let's say that you are looking through your email service, whether it is Gmail or some other kind. It is possible that you can use this in order to send things out to new customers and then gives you the ability to look through a new address as soon as it comes to your inbox. From that email, it would automatically take the information and place it into the address book. This helps you to keep that information in one place, save time, and ensures that you are not going to lose the information along the way.

Speech recognition

Another way that you are able to use machine learning is through speech recognition. This can be a hard one to work with because we have to consider the different sounds that each voice has, how the genders sound to one another, the different dialects that each person can use, speech patterns and fluctuations, and even different languages. The way that one person is going to say a word out loud is going to be completely different than the way someone else may decide to use or say it. And the program needs to be able to catch and learn how to recognize these different patterns.

A good example of a product that uses this is the Amazon Echo. On this program, machine learning is being used hardcore to help it be successful. This kind of program, along with the machine learning capabilities, are able to slowly learn the speech patterns of those who use it and then can use that information to respond in the proper manner. Of course, there are going to be some issues when you first get the device, and it is likely that it is going to give you the wrong result or not understand you. But as you use the device some more, and as machine learning programs get more advanced, this is going to become less of a problem.

Facial recognition

Machine learning is going to be able to help you out with facial recognition as well. This is going to require the system to work on several layers in order to figure out if the person in the picture is someone that it knows. This type would rely on photos as well as videos so that only the people who hold the right authorization would be able to use that system.

The system would look at these videos and photos and figure out who is allowed on the system. Through a series of learning processes, it would then tell who can get onto the system and who is not allowed there. If this is not set up the right way, then you may end up with those who are authorized not getting in and those without the proper authorization being able to get in. Machine learning will be able to provide you the tools that you need to get this done.

Just from this list, you can already see that there are a lot of things that machine learning will be able to help you out with. These are just some of the beginning options, the ones that have been used so far. But over time, as more people start to learn how to work with machine learning, and as more people start to accept that this is a great way to get their program to learn and develop more than anything else, it is likely that we are going to see more and more ways that this technology is going to grow.

Chapter 2: Is Artificial Intelligence the Same as Machine Learning?

The next topic that we need to explore here is the idea of artificial intelligence and whether it is seen as the same thing as machine learning. To someone who has just started reading through this guidebook, it may seem like machine learning, and artificial intelligence are the exact same thing. You may assume that we are talking about the same thing, or that they are pretty much the same thing, but this is just not true. There are actually some big differences that can occur between machine learning and artificial intelligence, and understanding the differences that show up between them, and how each one works is going to work can make a big difference in how you use them.

With machine learning, you will find that the process can work well when it comes to working with data science, and it can work in artificial intelligence as well. To start with, when we talk about the term of data science, it is a pretty broad thing to consider, and it will have a lot of different concepts that are included. But one of these concepts, to keep it simple, is machine learning. Other concepts though, will include data mining, big data, and artificial intelligence. Data science is really a filed that is growing since it is so new, and it won't take long before people find more and more uses for this topic.

Statistics is really important when it comes to data science, and it can also be used often when it comes to machine learning. You would be able to work with classical statistics, even at the higher levels, so that the data set is going to stay consistent throughout. But the way that you use it will depend on what kinds of data you are using and how complex the information gets.

It is important to understand the difference between the categories of artificial intelligence and machine learning. There are some instances where they can be very similar, but there are some major differences, which is why they are considered two different things. Let's take a look at each of these to ensure that we understand how they both work in data science.

What is artificial intelligence?

To help you figure out more about what machine learning and what artificial intelligence are, and how they are different, we are going to look at AI or artificial intelligence is all about. AI is a term that was first talked about in the 1950s thanks to John McCarthy. AI was first used in order to describe a method that you are able to use for manufactured devices in order to learn how to copy the capabilities of humans when it comes to some tasks that are mental.

The term is used in a bit different manner in our modern world, but the basic ideas are still the same with it. When you try to implement a program that uses AI, you will enable a machine, such as a computer, to operate and think in the same manner as a human brain can. This is something that is going to benefit you because not only will the AI device be able to think like a human; it is able to do it in a manner that is more efficient than the human brain is able to do.

When you are first getting started with these ideas, you may think that AI and machine learning are going to be the exact same thing. But there are some differences that come along. Some people who don't understand these two terms, and who don't understand how these terms work, may think that they are the same. But often the way that they are going to be used when it comes to the world of programming is what makes them so different and unique.

How is machine learning different?

Then there is machine learning. This option is going to be a bit newer than some of the other parts of data science, and it is just twenty years old. But even though machine learning has been around for this long, the last few years have really helped to bring this area into the limelight and computers are finally changing enough that you can use machine learning more and more.

When it comes to data science, machine learning is going to be the part that is able to specifically focus on having the program learn from any data input that it is given, and get better at making good predictions as well. The more the program is used, and the more the user is able to work with it, the better it will get at doing all of this work. For example, when you want to use the machine learning capabilities in a search engine, the user would put in some kind of term into the query. Then the search engine will provide you with some matching pages that you can choose from to find the information that you want.

When you first start using this option on the search engine, you will find that the query results are not going to be as accurate as you would like. You may have to search down to a lower result to find what you want, and it won't be at the top. But, the more you are able to do queries on the search engine, the better that engine is going to be at picking out the information that you want and providing you with better choices.

So, with this in mind, your first few times using that search engine, you may click on a result that is on the lower end of the page or you may have to move to the next page instead. But after you use this for a few weeks or more, you will be able to find the result that you want right at the top of the page.

If you have used traditional programming in the past, you may find that these codes are not able to do something like this. Each person is going to go through and put in different searches to their queries, even when they are looking for the same things. Plus, every person who is doing these kinds of searches online will have a preference when it comes to what they would like to pick out on the search engine. This makes it hard for them to work on a traditional code, but it is definitely something that machine learning is able to do, and it can do it in a successful manner.

Of course, the example of a search engine is just one of the things that are you are able to do when it comes to machine learning. There are actually a lot of different complex problems that you are able to do with your computer, thanks to machine learning. Sometimes, you will be able to work on these kinds of problems with the human brain, but you will often find that if you want to get it done quickly, and more efficiently, then the human brain is not the best for doing this, machine learning is.

Let's look at an example of when this would happen, and that will come with data mining. This often includes a lot of data, and often, this amount is so much and keeps coming in, that it is hard for a single person to go through in a timely or efficient manner. And if there is more than one person who comes in and tries to do it, the information can get mixed up, and there can be issues with missed information or misreading it. Having machine learning go through and check out that information, and then using that information to make predictions for the company based on that data will make a big difference in the speed and the accuracy.

Of course, it is possible if you would like to, it is possible to have someone go through this information and try to figure it all out to make predictions. But for larger companies, this is going to be a ton of information, and often too much for the person to do in an efficient manner. They could feel confused and overwhelmed about all of the information, they may not know the best way to search through all the information and start, and it is easy for them to miss out on some stuff when there is so much information.

Plus, when there are hundreds of thousands of data points to sift through, it can take the individual way too long to go through it, and the information could be outdated by the time they are done. Machine learning instead is going to be able to take on all of the work and can get the results and predictions back in a fraction of the time. This is why so many companies enjoy working with machine learning. They like to add this into their business model to help them understand their customers and make the right decisions for their futures.

Now that we have taken some time to learn more about machine learning, and how it is similar to and different from the ideas of artificial intelligence, you can see how these are completely different from one another. Now it is time to take that information and look at how to add in statistics to the mix and see more about how machine learning is able to work for you.

Chapter 3: Can I Use Probability and Statistics to Help Me with Machine Learning?

MACHINE LEARNING

As you start to work with the process of machine learning, it is important to know that there is going to be a nice relationship that ends up showing between this process, and what is called the probability theory. Machine learning is actually a pretty broad field to work with, and this means that it doesn't work just on its own, but also with some other fields at the same time. The fields that you will be able to work with often depend on the kind of project that you decide to start with.

One thing that you are going to notice when you start with machine learning is that it can merge together with statistics and probability. It is so important for a lot of the projects that you choose to start on to learn how these three different areas are going to work together.

Now, there are a few different methods that you can utilize with the probability and statistics, and all of them are important to the learning process that you need to see happen here. The first thing to consider is picking out the right algorithm. And as you go through this guidebook, you will find that there are actually a lot of different algorithms that you can use, including supervised, unsupervised, and reinforced learning algorithms as well. However, not all of the algorithms are going to work with every project that you have.

When you pick out one of the algorithms to work with (and we will talk about quite a few of these in this guidebook), there are a few things that you need to balance out together including the number of parameters that you need, the complexity, the training time that you can work with, and the accuracy. As we spend more time with machine learning, you will find that each project you need to focus on will ask for a certain combination of these factors, so consider that ahead of time.

When you decide to work with the ideas of statistics and the probability theory, you will be better prepared to pick out the parameters that are right for your specific program, the strategies for validation, and you can then use all of these in order to pick out the algorithm for this project. This is also going to be a helpful thing to use when you want to figure out the amount of uncertainty that is present in that algorithm, and then you can determine if there is a level of trust that you should have for any predictions.

As you can imagine here, both of these two topics are going to be very useful when it comes to working on any project with machine learning, and they will do wonders when you want to understand what is going on with any project. This chapter is going to spend some more time looking at the different topics that come with both statistics and the probability theory, and how you are able to use them on any project that you need.

What are the random variables?

Now, the first topic we need to look at when it comes to statistics is random variables. With probability theory, these random variables are going to be expressed with the "X" symbol, and it is the variable that has all its possible variables come out as numerical outcomes that will come up during one of your random experiments. With random variables, there are going to be either continuous or discrete options. This means that sometimes, your random variables will be functions that will map outcomes to the real value inside their space. We will look at a few examples of this one to help it make sense later on.

We are going to start out with an example of a random variable by throwing a die. The random variable that we are going to look at is going to be represented by X, and it will rely on the outcome that you will get once the die is thrown. The choices of X that would come naturally here is going to go through to map out the outcome denoted as 1 to the value of i.

What this means is that if X equals 1, you will map the event of throwing a one on your die to being the value of i. You would be able to map this out with any number that is on the die, and it is even possible to take it to the next step and pick out some mappings that are a bit strange. For example, you could map out Y to make it the outcome of 0. This can be a hard process to do, and we aren't going to spend much time on it, but it can help you to see how it works. When we are ready to write out his one, we would have the probability, which is shown as P of outcome 1 of random variable X. it would look like the following:

PX(i) or (x=i)

Distribution

Now that we have looked a bit at the random variables, it is time to look a bit at the idea of probability distribution and how it works with machine learning. What is meant here is that we need to take a look at the outcomes and figure out the probability that they are going to happen, or for a random variable to happen. To make this even easier, we are going to use this distribution to figure out how likely it is that we are going to get a specific number.

Let's say that you are working with a die. There are six sides on it, and you have a random probability of one of the numbers showing up each time that you throw it. We can use the distribution to figure out how likely it is that with a particular throw, we will get a five or a two or one of the other numbers.

To help us get started with this one, it helps to have an example. We will need to let the X, which is our random variable, but the outcome that we will see on the die when we throw it. We are also going to start out this kind of experiment using the assumption that the die is perfectly capable of being used, with no tricks and it isn't loaded. This ensures that the sides all end up with the same probability of showing up each time that you do a throw. The probability distribution that you will work with here to figure out how probable it is that one number will show up includes

$$PX(1) = PX(2) = \ldots = PX(6) = 1/6$$

In this example, it matches up to what we did with the random variables. It does have a different type of meaning. Your probability distribution is more about the spectrum of events that can happen, while our random variable example is all about which variables are there. With the probability theory, the P(X) part is going to note that we are working with our probability distribution of the random variable X.

While you take a look at this kind of example, you may notice that your distribution could have just one variable, or there could be two or more of these variables that show up at the same time. When you do see this occur, you will name it a joint distribution. In order to figure out this kind of probability, you will need to figure out the variables on their own and combine them together to see the results.

To see how this is going to work when it comes to two or more variables, let's have X be the random variable and the one that will be defined by the outcome you can get any time you throw the die. And then you are able to use Y to show us the random variable that will tell you what results occur if you decide to flip a coin. For this one, to make things easier, we are going to assign the heads side of the coin 1 and the tails side is going to be 0. This is just used in order to help us figure out the probability distribution for each variable on their own and together.

We are going to denote this joint distribution as $P(X, Y)$ and the probability of X as having an outcome of a and Y as having an outcome of b as either $P(x = a, Y = b)$ or $P_{X,Y}(a,b)$.

Conditional distribution

The next thing that we need to bring into the mix with machine learning and statistics is the idea of conditional distribution. When we already know what the random variable distribution is all about, possibly because we already know the value of the second random variable, then we are able to base the probability of one event based on the outcome that we can get with that second event. So, you will find that when you use this kind of distribution, you will have the random variable be known as X when X -2 given that the variable of Y is going to be Y = b. When these are true, the following formula is going to help you to define and figure out what the variable is for both of the situations:

$$P(X = a \mid Y = b) = P(X = a, Y = b)/P(Y = b).$$

As you work through machine learning, there are going to be a few times when you may need to use conditional distributions. These can be good tools depending on the system that you are designing, especially if you need to have the program reason with uncertainty.

Independence

And finally, the last thing that we need to take a look at when it comes to working with statistics and probability during machine learning is independence. One of the variables that you can work with here is to figure out how much independence there is inside the problem. When you work with these kinds of random variables, you are going to find out that they are going to be independent of what the other random variables are, as long as the distribution that you have doesn't change if you take a new variable and try to add it into that equation.

To make this one work a bit better, you are going to need to work with a few assumptions in concerns to the data that you are using with machine learning. This makes it a bit easier when you already know about independence. A good example to help us understand what this is all about is a training sample that uses j and I and are independent of any underlying space when the label of sample I is unaffected by the features sample j. no matter what one of the variables turns out, the other one is not going to see any change or be affected, if they are independent.

Think back to the example of the die and the coin flip. It doesn't matter what number shows up on the die. The coin is going to have its own result. And the same can be said the other way around as well. The X random variable is always going to be independent of the Y variable. It doesn't matter the value of Y, but the following code needs to be true for it:

$P(X) = P(X|Y)$.

In the case above, the values that come up for X and for Y variables are dropped because, at this point, the values of these variables are not going to matter that much. But with the statement above, it is true for any type of value that you provide to your X or Y, so it isn't going to matter what values are placed in this equation.

This chapter went over just a few of the things that you can do with the help of probability theory and statistics when you are working on machine learning. You are able to experiment with some of these to get the hang of what you can do with the use of them, and then we can learn a few more algorithms that you can use later on.

Chapter 4: How Do I Learn the Building Blocks to Be Successful with Machine Learning?

Before we start to take a look at the different types of machine learning algorithms that are out there, and we divide them up into the three main sections to make things easier, we need to take a look at some of the building blocks that are so important when it comes to doing well with machine learning.

There are going to be some important algorithms that you will want to learn all about and how to use to ensure that you see the best results with any projects you do in machine learning. Before we get into those and more about when and how to use them, it is important to learn a few of the basic building blocks of machine learning to make things easier. Doing this is going to really help you when you are ready to work with any of these algorithms.

As you learn more about this process and get more into making your own projects, you will find that these algorithms are going to be so awesome to work with. These algorithms, when you use them properly, are able to do a lot of amazing things when it comes to machine learning. And they are often seen as the main reason why you would want to use this process.

But before we get to all of these algorithms and explore all of the amazing things that come with it, we need to learn a few basics of machine learning. These will include things like learning the framework that comes with machine learning, and some of the underlying topics that will make sure you see the results that you want.

The learning framework

If you remember back to the previous chapter, you will most likely remember that we spent some time talking about all of the statistics that often go with machine learning. When you use some of the contexts that we spent time on before, it is easier to simplify the whole process of learning that your computer will need to go through. If this sounds confusing, let's look at an example to help us get started.

For this example, let's say that you want to visit a new island and go on a vacation. You go there, and the natives from there seem like they enjoy eating some papaya on a regular basis. You want to have some to try as well and would like to enjoy it as well, but since your experience with this food is limited, it is hard to know which ones are going to taste good, and which ones you won't like. But, despite this, you still want to give it a try, and you make your way to the marketplace in the hopes of figuring out the best tasting one.

There are a few different options that you are able to use in order to look at the papayas and figure out the one that is going to work the best for you, the one that you like the taste of the best. You could start out this process by going down to the marketplace and asking around, finding out the opinion of those around to see if you will find the right one. Of course, for each person you ask, you are likely to get a lot of answers as well.

Another option to rely on is your own experiences with fruits in the past. At one point or another, you have purchased some fruit at the store. You probably have a method that you like to use to make picking out the fruit a bit easier. You could use these same ideas to help you look through the papaya that is available at the market, and make your decision.

Once you get to the supermarket, you can take a look at the papaya, maybe noticing the color, and the softness of the fruit to make the best decisions. As you take a look at these fruits though, you will notice that they come in many different colors from reds to browns. And they have a variety when it comes to how soft and hard they are. This can make it even more confusing to know what is going to work or not.

So, you look around to see what is there, and in the process, you decide to come up with a model to help you learn the best papaya so you are prepared for the next time you come to the market. This model that you are going to make here, which is in a simplified form with the fruits, will be known as a formal statistical learning framework. There will be four components that we are going to focus on with this framework, and they include:

1. Some simple data generalization
2. A measure of how successful it is
3. The output from the learner
4. And the input from the learner

Each of these four parts will be important when it comes to helping us to figure out which type of papaya we like the most. And the more variety and information you feed to this in the beginning, the more accurate your results are going to be the next time that you head to the marketplace. Let's take a look at what each of these components is all about so you can make the right decisions.

The input of the learner

The first section of the framework that you need to look at is called the learner's input. To do this, you need to find a domain set and then focus on it. This domain can be an arbitrary set that is found in the objects, which in this framework is known as the points, that you need to get labeled. So, going back to the exercise about the papaya, you would have the domain set be any of the papayas that you are checking out. Then the domain points would be able to use the vectors of features, which in this case includes the softness and color of the fruit.

Once you have determined what domain points and domain sets you want to use, you can then go through and create the label set that you will use. In this exercise, the label set is going to hold onto the predictions that you will make about the papayas. You can look at each papaya and then make a prediction on how it tastes and whether it is the best one for you.

The label set that you get with this exercise is going to have two elements. The X is going to be any of the papayas that you think are going to taste bad. And then the Y is going to be the ones that you feel taste the best.

From here, you can work on what is known as the training data. This training data is going to be a set which can hold the sequence pairs that you will use when testing the accuracy of your predictions. So, with the exercise of the papayas, the training data will be the papayas that you decide to purchase. You will then take these home, and taste them to see what tastes the best. This can help you to make better decisions later on when you purchase papayas. If you find that you really like a specific softness or color, you will ensure that you purchase kind the next time.

The output of the learner

Once you have gone through and figured out the input of your learner, it is time to figure out what your output will be, based on that same input. This output is going to be used to help you create a prediction on what you will like and what you will want to avoid. There are a few different names that you may hear it called, including classifier, predictor, and hypothesis, and you are going to use these in order to take the domain points and label them.

So, going back to the example that we have done with the papaya, this rule is going to be the standard, which you are going to set at the best place for you. You can then use this standard to make it easier to figure out whether any given papaya is going to taste good or not before you purchase it the next time you head to the market.

Now, when you decide to get started with this, you are just making some guesses. You have never had papaya before, so figuring out which one is the best will take some trial and error. Of course, it is perfectly fine to bring in some of the experiences that you have from the past to help out with this if you would like. But, given the fact that you haven't had papaya in the past, you may be wrong about your assumptions in the beginning.

The best way for this example to get output is to make some guesses based on your past experiences with fruits, and then take a bite and see if you were right. If you can pick out a lot of different papayas, and try out a bite or two of each one, you will quickly be able to figure out which one tastes the best to you, and from there you can look at the characteristics of it and make a decision based on that.

Using the data generalization model

Once you have gone through this example, or any machine learning example that you would like to work with, and you have figured out what the input and the output of the learner is going to be, it is time to work with the data generalization model. This is a nice model to work with because it will ensure you are able to create some training data to use, and this data is going to be based on the probability distribution of the domain sets that you decide to use with the papayas.

We are still sticking with the papayas here. In this example, you will find that the model you need to focus on is going to be any method that you would like to use to help you figure out the best-tasting papaya. It can help you to figure out what to grab at the market so you can bring home some variety and figure out what tastes good for later.

Of course, the distribution is hard to figure out when you have never worked with papaya, or with the given data, in the past. But using this data generalization model is going to help you get a better distribution of the data, and can make it easier to pick out the right kinds of papaya, right from the beginning.

How to measure the success

Now, while the data generalization model is a great one to work with, you are not able to work with this kind of model until you have found a way to measure out whether you were successful or not. You need to put in place a method that will make it easier to know whether or not you were successful with this particular product.

The good news with this is that there are quite a few options that are available for you to choose from with this. But since there are a good number of options in papayas to choose from, you need to have some indicator in place along the way that can help with predictions and will help you to see success when it is time to make your selections.

Remember that the main goal that comes with this experiment is to help you as the user figure out, from all of the different options, the fruit that will taste the best. When you figure this out, you will be able to keep that information in mind to pick out the right papayas to use in the future.

Since there is a good deal of variety when it comes to the softness, the shape, and the color of the papaya, you may find that picking out a good sample, different softness and different colors can be the best bet for you here. You can then taste each one, and write down what your observations were with each of them so that you are more likely to head back and grab the right ones the next time if you choose.

If you go through this and only grab one or two of the fruits, and there are twenty different kinds there, you are reducing the odds that you are going to be able to find a type that you like. Maybe none of those two taste good. Maybe they taste fine to you, but there is one in the mix that would taste even better, but you haven't had a chance to taste it yet. This is why having a wide sample size can make it more likely that you will get accurate results.

PAC strategies of learning

Now that we know the four main components that come with the idea of machine learning, and we know how to set up our hypothesis and how to set up your own training data, it is time to look at something that is known as PAC learning. There are going to be two main parameters that are important to this kind of learning and they include the output classifier and the accuracy parameter.

To help us get started with this one we need to focus on the accuracy parameter first. This parameter is important because it is going to be used by the user to determine how often the output classifier that you are setting up, in the beginning, will be able to make predictions that are the right ones. You need to have these predictions set up so that they can look at the information that you are providing and then the predictions are based back on these.

You can also take some time to work on the confidence parameter when you are in machine learning. This is another important parameter because it is the one that will measure how likely it is that your predictor will be able to reach the level of accuracy that you would like. Depending on the kind of data that you are using, and the situation that you find yourself in, accuracy is going to be really important. You want to make sure that any kind of algorithm you choose to go with is able to be fairly high when it comes to accuracy. Otherwise, how are you supposed to know that your information is true or that it will work out the best for your needs?

As you work with machine learning, you will find that there are several different ways that you can utilize these PAC learning options and they can really come in handy when you are doing a project. You may want to use this kind of learning any time you work with training data to help you see whether you are getting the accuracy you want. You may want to use it and have it go along with machine learning when you are worried about uncertainties that will come up in the data.

The PAC strategies for learning in machine learning are going to be very useful when it comes to helping you to get the results that you would like out of the project. We will take a look at a few algorithms that will work well with this as we progress through this book, but learning the basics of them now can prepare you when your project needs this kind of thing to show up.

Generalization models that can help out with machine learning

Any time that you are working with machine learning, and you are considering all about the generalization of the project, you are basically going through and seeing that there are at least two components present there, and that you need to work with both of these components before you can accurately and efficiently get through the data that you have. the components that you really need to focus on for these generalizations include the rate of error that is true and the reliability assumption.

One thing that you should look for is whether or not you are able to work with those two components and you are also able to meet with the reliability assumption, it is a good thing. When these happen together, you are able to expect that the algorithm you are using here is going to be reliable and will give you the distribution and the results that you would like.

With that said, there are also going to be times when the assumption that you try to make with these generalizations ends up not being all that practical. This means that the standards you ended up picking may have turned out unrealistic, or that you actually went through and chose the wrong algorithm when it was time to get the work done.

There are a lot of different algorithms that you can focus on when you are doing machine learning. And the type that you decide to go with on one of your projects doesn't always guarantee that the hypothesis that it comes up with will turn out to be something that you agree with or like. Unlike using the Bayes predictor (which we will talk about more in a bit), which is a good algorithm to use for many of the predictions that you want to make, these algorithms are not going to be set up in the right way for you to find out which type of error rate is the best.

You have to choose the algorithm that you want to use very carefully. There are some projects that you will want to focus on that have a really set and easy algorithm. You can look at it and know right away what algorithm you should use. But then there are some of those projects that more than one will work, or you have to figure out which one is going to work the best, and this is where some trouble can come in.

Sometimes, there isn't a cut and dry answer that you are able to work with, and you just have to make an educated guess as to which one is going to work the best for you. And then there are times when you will need to try out two of them and figure out whether they cross over at some point, and use that as your basis here. As you get more into machine learning, you will be able to learn what works the best for you, and you can continue to use this on any project that you want.

When you are doing anything in machine learning, there will be times, no matter how hard you try to fight against it or hope that it doesn't happen, that you will need to make some assumptions to move things along. And in these cases, working with the experience that you already have, the ones that are similar to what you are dealing with now, can help to move the process along and get accurate results. And then, like with the example of our papayas above, you may have some times when you need to experiment to figure out what is the best course of action. But no matter which method or algorithm or anything else that you need to go with, you will be able to use machine learning to make this easier.

And there you have it! These are some of the most basic building blocks that you will need to know when it is time to understand more about machine learning. Keeping these in mind, and reviewing them before you decide to start on some of your own projects, will help you to get the most out of your machine learning experience.

These basic building blocks may sound like they are going to be a waste of time, and you may not understand how they are going to work in your projects, they are so important here. You will be able to work with these simple building blocks in order to see how programs that are run thanks to machine learning are really working. You will then be able to see how this information is used in the following chapters as we talk more about some of the algorithms that are used in machine learning.

Chapter 5: What Is Supervised Machine Learning?

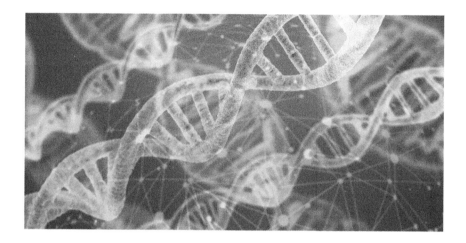

So far in this guidebook, we have spent some time talking about machine learning and some of the neat things that you are able to do with it. Now that we have some of the basics down about machine learning and how to use it, it is time to move on to some of the types of machine learning you can work with, and even some of the algorithms that work well with this as well.

To start out with, in this chapter there are three main types of machine learning that programmers are able to use. The three main types, including the one we will explore in this chapter, include supervised, unsupervised, and reinforcement learning. All of these are going to be a part of machine learning, but they are going to work in different ways to help you get the results that you need for your project. The one type that you will want to work with often depends on the type of project, as you will see as we explore them a bit more.

First, we need to take a look at the most basic type of machine learning known as supervised machine learning. Supervised learning is the type that will occur when you choose one of the algorithms that can learn the right responses to any data that is given to it. There are a few different ways that supervised machine learning is able to work with this. You may find that supervised learning an look at an example, along with some other targeted responses, that you set to the computer. You could also spend some time adding values or other strings of labels to help the program learn the way that you want it to behave.

This is a pretty simple process that you can work with. But a good way to look at this is when we look at a classroom. A teacher may choose to show their students a brand new topic, and one method of doing this is to show the class of students some examples of the situation that is going on.

Through this method, the students are going to learn how to memorize these examples because they know that these examples are going to provide them with some general rules to follow. Any time they see these examples, along with other examples that are similar to what they were shown, they know how to respond. However, if they see an example that isn't similar to what they were shown in class, they also know how to respond in this situation as well.

There are several types of learning algorithms you are able to use when it comes to supervised machine learning. But the most common types and the ones that we are going to explore in this chapter will include:

1. Random forests
2. Regression algorithms

3. KNN

4. Decision trees

Decision trees

The first algorithm we are going to take a look at with supervised machine learning is the decision trees. These are nice to work with because they are efficient data tools any time that you would like to look at the different scenarios that are provided, and then pick out the right options for these for your business. Once the decision tree is able to present you with a few options, you can see the outcomes and the possibilities that come with them. And all of this information can be used in order to help you make predictions that are the most accurate and helpful for your needs.

It is also possible to use these decision trees for either continuous random variables, or when you want to work with categorical variables. However, most of the time, when you decide to work with these decision trees, you are working with classification problems.

In order for a programmer to make a good decision tree, it is important to take all of the data and split it up into domains, and then you will split it up into a minimum of two sets, even though you will often get more, of similar data. These data sets are going to be sorted out with the help of their independent variables because it will make it easier to distinguish the different sets that you are working with as well.

So, we have talked about these a bit here, but it is time to get a better idea of how this works. For this example, we are going to assume that there are 60 people in the group. Out of these people in the group, there are going to be three independent variables to consider including their gender, which class they are in, and their heights.

When we take a look at all of these people in the group, we know from the start that half of them, or 30 people, like to spend some of their time playing soccer. So, with this knowledge, we decide to work on a model that will help us to better figure out which of the students are soccer players and enjoy playing this sport, and which ones aren't.

To help us to figure this out, we need to work on a decision tree, one that is able to look at the people in the group and divide them up based on their similarities and more. We would use the three variables that we talked about before. If the decision tree works out the way that we would like, or hope is that we are going to find a set of students that can end up homogenous when it is all said and done.

Of course, there are some other algorithms that you are able to use to figure this one out. And some of them ware going to work well with the decision tree to ensure that you can accurately split up the data that you have. This is to ensure that you are going to end up with two subsets at a minimum and that the outcomes of both of these subsets are going to end up homogenous. It is possible to have more of these, but since we are just trying to figure out whether we have a person in the group who likes to play soccer or not, right now we are just going to work on dividing the students up into two groups, whether they play soccer or not.

Decision trees can be a great option for you to work with when it comes to supervised machine learning. This is because these decision trees will allow you to take the data and split them up. Then, with this data split up and ready to go, you can look it over and make some decisions. It is a great way to ensure that you are making the best decisions for your business and for yourself, because all of the information is going to be in front of you, sorted out and easy to read, rather than having to look at all of the conflicting information and make an educated guess in the process.

Random forests

There are a lot of situations where you are able to use the decision tree to make some of the decisions and to sort the data that you want. But there are also times when it just isn't going to do the work the right way. If you are looking at your data and you know that the decision tree isn't the right option for you, then you may find that the random forest is a bit better to work with.

These random forests can be popular to use, and if you plan to do a lot of work in the field of data science, then you definitely will want to learn more about these and how you can use them in your needs. Since these algorithms are well-known in the industry and popular, you will find that many people use them to solve out various problems that come up. For example, if you would like to work on a task that will explore through all the data you have, such as dealing with some of the values that may have gone missing, or dealing with any of the information outliers that show up, these random forests are going to be there to help you get it all done.

Now, you may find that as you work on machine learning, there will be some times when you will use them because they seem to be the perfect option for giving you great results, results that other algorithms are just not able to do. Some of the different advantages that you are able to get when it comes to these random forests will include:

1. When you decide to create some of your own training sets and to work on these, you may find that all of the objects that are inside that set will be generated in a random manner. You will be able to replace this if your

random tree works the right way, and can help you to sort through the information based on your needs.

2. If there are M input variable amounts, then m<M is going to be specified from the beginning, and it will be held as a constant. The reason that this is so important because it means that each tree that you have is randomly picked from their own variable using M.

3. The goal of each of your random trees will be to find the split that is the best for the variable m.

4. As the tree grows, all of these trees are going to keep getting as big as they possibly can. Remember that these random trees are not going to prune themselves.

5. The forest that is created from a random tree can be great because it is much better at predicting certain outcomes. It is able to do this for you because it will take all prediction from each of the trees that you create and then will be able to select the average for regression or the consensus that you get during classification.

You may find that it is great to work with random forests any time that you are doing things in data science, and there are going to be quite a few advantages to working with a random forest rather than some of the other algorithms, even though it isn't going to be perfect each time. just because the random variable can provide you with a lot of the results that you would like, you do have to know when it can be useful and when it should be avoided. With that said, there are some advantages to its use.

First, these random forests are good to use because they can work with regression and classification problems that you have. Many other algorithms are not able to work with both of these. In addition, you may find that random forests are a good option to go with if you are handling large amounts of data because you can add in hundreds of data points and variables, and the random forest will still be able to handle this.

One thing to consider when you are working with this is that while the random forest is able to handle a lot of regression problems, they will have some issues when it comes to making predictions. Random forests are not going to be limited in this because they are not able to go past any of the ranges that you provide to them so there may be times when your accuracy is not going to be as high as you would like.

The KNN algorithm

The third type of supervised machine learning algorithm that you are able to work with is known as the KNN algorithm. This one is also known as the k-nearest neighbor's algorithm. When you decide to use this algorithm, it is going to be helpful to take all of your data, the data that you have for k most similar examples of any instance of data that you are working on. Once you see some success with this, the KNN algorithm will then be able to go through all of your data points and can provide you with a summary of all the results. Many companies and programmers are able to use this to help them look through the results and make some good predictions.

Any time that you plan to work with this KNN algorithm model, you will be able to see it as a form of competitive learning. This is going to work well because the different elements will end up competing against one another. This may sound like a bad thing, but when the elements start to compete against one another, they become better at making predictions that are successful.

As you can imagine, this one is going to work a bit different than the other algorithms that we have talked about in this guidebook so far. There are some programmers who don't like to use it because they think that KNN is more of a lazy learning process. This is because while it can be effective at providing you with some results, it isn't going to help you out by creating any models until you specifically ask it for a brand new prediction. This can be good sometimes, but it will depend on the case. Some people want it to make new predictions automatically, and some like that they will have the most relevant information for the task at hand.

There are different benefits that can come when you decide to work with this KNN algorithm. When you choose to go with this algorithm, you can cut through a lot of the noise that is found inside your specific set of data. This is because the KNN algorithm is going to rely more on a competitive method to sort through all of the data that you see. This algorithm is going to be great when you want to handle a lot of data, so it is definitely one that you should consider if your data is pretty large. At the same time, it works well if you need some help sorting through all of this data.

Now, you could have someone go through and look at all this information, providing you with some estimations and predictions for you as well. But this is not that efficient with really large forms of data. Sure, it can be done, but it can take a long time, often so long that new data is coming in and the predictions you have will be too old to work with. It can also lead to more mistakes as someone could miss information or misread it as well. The KNN algorithm can solve this problem by taking out the human error and sorting through any amount of data that you would like.

One of the biggest problems that you are going to see when you decide to work with the KNN algorithm is that the costs of computing the information are going to be pretty high, especially when you try to compare it to some of the algorithms that are there. This is because this kind of algorithm is meant to take a look at all of the data points that you have, each and every one before it sends out the prediction that you want. This sometimes provides more accurate predictions and information, but the computational costs may be too high for some people.

The Naïve Bayes

The next type of machine learning that we are going to take a look at here is known as the Naïve Bayes. To start this one, let's turn on our imaginations a bit to help us to really understand how this one is going to work. Here, we need to imagine that we are doing some machine learning work, and our scenario is going to be that we need to do problems of classification. In the process, we want to be able to create a brand new hypothesis as well as design some new discussions and features that will be based on the importance that we give to each variable.

Once we have been able to gather and use this information, it is likely that, even though it is early on in the process, the stakeholders of that company are going to want to look at the models and see what is going on. Of course, at this early of a stage, it is not likely that you will have that information ready to present. So, how are you supposed to make the stakeholders happy and provide them with the information that they want if you aren't done with it yet?

In many cases, you are starting out this process with hundreds of thousands of data points that you need to go through, and all of these need to be shown in the model. In addition to this, there are going to be a lot of other variables that can show up in this kind of training set as well. This is a lot of information to throw together quickly, especially if you haven't been able to sort through it all. And it is likely that your stakeholders are not data scientists and won't be able to read through all of that information just by having you throw it on a screen in front of them. How are you able to take this information and show it to your stakeholders and present it in a way they will understand.

The good news is with this scenario, there is a good algorithm that a data scientist is able to work with to help out, and can ensure that you are able to stick with some of the earlier stages of the model, while still showing the information off in a manner that is easy for others to understand. And all of this can be done while showing all of the information that you need. The algorithm that works the best for this is going to be called the Naïve Bayes algorithm, and it is one of the best ways to use a few demonstrations to showcase your model, even when you are still in some of the earliest stages of development.

Let's take a look at how this is going to be able to work by looking at an example with apples. When you grab a normal looking apple, you should be able to state some of the features that are the most distinguishable about it. This could include that your apple is red or green, that it is sort of round, and it is going to come in around three inches. While some of these features are going to be found in other fruit types as well, when all of these features are present together, then we know how the fruit we are holding is a fruit.

Now, this may seem to be a pretty basic way to think and look at things, but it is a good way to understand how the Naïve Bayes formula is going to work. The model of Naïve Bayes is meant to be easy for anyone, whether they are a programmer or not, to put together, and sometimes it is going to be used in order to help you look through large data sets in a simple manner. Sometimes it is easier to work with this model compared to some of the other models out there, even if they are more sophisticated.

As you start to learn more about machine learning and the Naïve Bayes algorithm, you will find that there were going to be a lot of reasons and situations when you will use it. This model is really easy to use, and it is effective when it comes to predicting the class of your test data sets, so it is a great choice for someone who wants to keep things simple or who is new to the whole process. Even though this kind of a simple algorithm to use, this model is still going to perform well, and it has proven that it is able to do a job that is better than some of the higher class algorithms in some cases.

You do need to be careful with this one though because there are some negatives to using the Naïve Bayes' algorithm. First, when you are working with categorical variables, and you need to test data that hasn't been through the training data set, you will find that this model is not able to make a good prediction for you and will assign those data sets a 0 probability. You can add in some other methods that will help to solve this issue, such as the Laplace estimation, but it can be confusing for someone who is brand new to working in machine learning.

This is not going to be the method that you use all of the time, but if you have a lot of information that you are working on, and you need to be able to showcase it in a simplified manner for your shareholders or for anyone else, then working with the Naïve Bayes algorithm is the best option for you.

Regression algorithms

Another algorithm that works well when you are working with machine learning is called a regression analysis. This is going to be the type that you can use when you want to look through your predictor variables and any dependent variables and whether there is a relationship between them. You will see that this is a good technique that you can work with when you want to figure out if there is a causal relationship between the variable, the time series modeling, and the forecasting that you are using.

The point of using a regression algorithm is that it should take all of the information that you have and fits it on a line or a curve, as much as it can. This helps you to see the common factors that show up in your data. This is a good way to help you figure out whether there are some similarities that show up in your information or data points or not.

There are many companies who will use the regression algorithm in order to help them make great predictions that will increase their profits. You will be able to use it in order to come up with a great estimation of the sales growth for the company while still basing it on how the economic conditions in the market are doing right at this moment.

The great thing about this is that you are able to add in any information that you would like to use. You can add in information about the past and the current economy to this particular algorithm, such as your past and current economic information, and then this gives you an idea of how the growth is going to go in the future. Of course, you do need to have the right information about the company to make this happen.

For example, if you use the regression algorithm and find that your company is growing at the same rate as what other industries are doing in the economy, you would then be able to use this information to help make predictions for how your company will do in the future if the economy does end up changing.

As you are working with this kind of algorithm in machine learning, there are going to be a few variations of it that you may enjoy. You have to learn how each one is able to be used, so you know whether or not it will work for your particular project or not. There are many variations of this algorithm that are available for you to use, but some of the most common options are going to include:

1. Stepwise regression
2. Ridge regression
3. Polynomial regression
4. Linear regression
5. Logistic regression

When you are working with these regression algorithms, you will easily be able to take a look to see that there is a nice relationship present with your dependent and your independent variables. This algorithm is also going to help you to know what kind of impact will show up if you try to add in or change some of the variables that show up in the data.

Even though this is a great option to work with, it is important to note that there are a few shortcomings that will show up with it. The biggest shortcoming that can often come up with this is that this algorithm is not very good at helping with classification problems. The main reason for this one is that it is too hard to try and overfit the data that you have in many situations. So, any time that you would like to change up the constraints that you are using with this, the whole process is going to be tedious to get done.

As you can see from this chapter, there are actually quite a few different algorithms that you are able to use when it comes to machine learning, even when you are using the supervised machine learning variety. These are going to be pretty simple ones, where you teach the computer how to behave and work up from there. The computer or the program will then be able to use some of the information that it has gathered throughout the time, and from the past, to make informed predictions about what will happen in the future.

Supervised machine learning does have some parts that are lacking, but you will find that it is a great way to help you ensure that the program is able to do some of the learning that it needs on its own, and the type of algorithm that you are going to use will really depend on the application and the project you have to get done. After reading through this chapter, you should have a better idea of whether this is the right type of machine learning algorithm for you, and which one would actually be able to help you out here.

Chapter 6: Unsupervised Machine Learning

Now that we have had some time to explore a bit about supervised machine learning, it is time to move on to some of the other options that you can work with when it comes to machine learning. The first one that we spent some time talking about was supervised learning. As we discussed, supervised learning is designed in a way where you will show the computer some examples, and then you teach that computer how you would like it to respond based on the examples that you decide to show it.

There are going to be a lot of programs where this kind of technique is going to end up working well for you. But, when you think about showing hundreds or thousands of different examples to your computer, it is all going to seem pretty tedious. And then there are times when the program isn't going to be able to learn this way and still give you the results that you are looking for. This is where the other two types of machine learning are going to come into play.

This is where you will find unsupervised machine learning is going to come into play. This chapter is going to spend some more time talking about unsupervised machine learning and what it is all about. Unsupervised machine learning is going to be a type of learning that is going to happen if your algorithm makes mistakes and is able to learn from these mistakes along the way. And the program is able to do it even without having an associated response to work from.

This may sound a bit confusing, but it is basically going to be when you are able to teach the computer through trial and error, without it having to work with a million examples to make sure it behaves how you would like it to do. With these different algorithms, it is possible that they are able to figure out and analyze the patterns in the data based on any kind of input that you and the user provide to it.

The good news here is that there are going to be a few different algorithm types that you are able to work with when you decide to choose unsupervised machine learning. The algorithm that you choose to work with is going to be able to take the data that you have, and it will restructure it so that the data can fall into one of your classes.

These classes are nice because they make it easier for you to see the information nice and sorted out, and it makes it so much easier for you to look through the information later on. There are many times when you will use this kind of machine learning because it is able to set up your computer, or another device, to do most of the work of learning, without having a person sit there and writing out all of the instructions. The computer will do some trial and error and figure out how it should act over time.

Let's take a look at an example of how this is going to work. If you have a company that has a huge amount of data that they want to read through, such as data that they want to use in order to make predictions and make decisions about how to act in the future, then you may want to work with machine learning. You don't want to have one or two people go through this information. It would take up too much time and effort to get this all done. But unsupervised machine learning is going to be able to do the work for you. Search engines often use unsupervised machine learning as well.

Working with unsupervised learning

Before we get too far into some of the techniques that can be used with unsupervised machine learning, it is important to understand a little bit about it. When you are working in a real-world environment, there are going to be times when your machine, either in artificial intelligence or a robotic role, won't be able to access the optimal answer with the information that you provided. Maybe there isn't even an optimal answer to the question that was asked. You want to make sure that this robot or machine is able to explore the world all on its own, and that it can learn how to do things just by taking a look at the patterns available.

In most cases, unsupervised learning is for learning the structure, or even the probability distribution of data. But what does this mean? We are going to spend some time talking about some of the different examples where you are able to use unsupervised learning to help get things done.

There are a few different ways that you will be able to work with unsupervised learning. Often it is to help the computer or the machine to find the answers or the results that you want, without you having to explain it out. With unsupervised learning, the computer is going to learn how to behave based on past performance and the feedback that it received. This can be nice because you will be able to insert the information that you want, and the computer will do the work.

Density Estimation

You should know at this point that we use the probability density function, or PDF, to tell us the probability that will occur of a random variable. Density estimation is the process of taking samples of data of the random variable and figuring out the probability density function. After you are able to learn the distribution of the variable, you will be able to use machine learning in order to generate your own samples of the variable based on this information.

For example, at a higher level, you could take Shakespeare and learn its distribution. You can then take this information and generate out a text that looks very similar to what you would find with Shakespeare.

Latent Variables

Many times, you will want to know some of the underlying or the hidden causes of the data you are looking at. You can consider these hidden, missing, or latent variable. For example, say that someone gives you a set of documents, but they don't tell you what these documents are. You would be able to use the clustering option with machine learning in order to find out that there are a few distinct groups of information in the document. The machine learning would be able to tell you this information rather than you having to read through it all.

After you have done clustering, you can read through a few of the documents in this data set and find out that maybe one is children's books, one is romance novels, and so on. There are several different types of clustering that you are able to work with. You would use this information any time when the data is just too big that it doesn't make sense for you to go through all of it on your own. The clustering process will be able to summarize the data to help you sort it all out.

There are a few different techniques that you are able to use when it is time to work with machine learning of this kind. Some of the methods or the algorithms that tend to work the best here are going to include:

1. Neural networks
2. Markov algorithm
3. Clustering algorithm

Let's explore each of these topics and learn a bit more about how they are all going to work, and some of the basics of when and how you are going to be able to use them for your own needs with machine learning.

Clustering algorithms

The first type of machine learning that we will look at is called the clustering algorithm. With the clustering algorithm, we are going to keep it pretty simple. This method is able to take our data and then classify it into clusters. Before the program even starts, you get the benefit of picking out how many clusters you would like all the information to fit into. For example, you may decide that you want to combine the data into five different clusters. The program would then go through and divide up all the information that you have into five different clusters so that you could look through it.

The nice thing about this algorithm is that it is responsible for doing most of the work for you. This is because it is in charge of how many of your data points are going to fit into those clusters that you chose. To keep things organized, we are going to call all of the main clusters that you picked cluster centroids.

So, when you are looking at one of your clusters, and you notice that there are a lot of points inside of it, you can safely make the assumption that all those particular data points have something in common or they are similar. There is some attribute or another that all the data points in one cluster have in common with each other.

Once these original clusters are formed, you can take each of the individual ones and divide them up to get more cluster sets if you would like. You can do this several times, creating more divisions as you go through the steps. In fact, you could potentially go through this enough times that the centroids will stop changing. This is when you know you are done with the process.

There are several reasons why you would want to work with a clustering algorithm to help you get a program started when doing machine learning. First, doing your computations with the help of a clustering algorithm can be easy and cost efficient, especially compared to some of the supervised learning options that we talked about before. If you would like to do a classification problem, the clustering algorithms are efficient at getting it done.

With that said, you do need to use some caution here though. This algorithm is not going to be able to do the work of showing predictions for you. If you end up with centroids that are not categorized the right way, then you may end up with a project that is done the wrong way.

Markov algorithm

The next type of unsupervised machine learning that you can work with is going to be the Markov algorithm. This is a nice one to use because it is able to take any and all of the data that you add to the system, and then it translates this information so that it is able to work with another coding language. You will be able to set this up with any and all of the rules that you would like to be present ahead of time, based on how you would like this to work. There are times when doing this is going to be useful because it can take a string of data and make it more useful when you learn the parameters for how your data is going to behave.

There are a lot of different ways that you are able to work with this Markov algorithm. One option that is available is if you decide to do some work with DNA. You would be able to take some of the DNA sequences that you have and use this particular algorithm in order to take that information and translate it over to numerical values. When you are working with this on a computer, you will find that reading out numerical values is going to be so much easier compared to looking at a random strand of DNA and hoping that you will be able to read through it.

You will find that a lot of programmers like to work with the Markov algorithm. A good reason to start using this one is that it is so great at learning some of the problems that you need, especially when you know the right input to use, but you are not sure about the parameters. This type of algorithm will help you to find if there are any insights that are found in your information. There are going to be times when these important insights are hidden, and this is when other algorithms are going to run into issues finding them.

There are a lot of neat things that come with this algorithm, but there are also going to be some downfalls that come with it as well. There are some instances where it is difficult to work with this one because you will need to go through manually and create a new rule to use any time that you are working with a new language of code. If you only plan to use one kind of coding language in your program, then this is not going to end up causing any issues along the way. but there are times when one program is going to need a lot of different coding languages, or you will want to work with more than one, then you will run into some trouble here and need to do some work with it. It can get tedious to come through and write out some new rules each time that you want to introduce in a new coding language.

Neural networks

The next type of unsupervised machine learning that we are going to talk about is known as neural networks. These are going to be the networks that are used often in this because they are able to learn things really quickly, and they are good at taking a look at a pattern and analyzing it at different layers along the way. Each layer that the neural network analyzes will be dissected and will look through it to figure out what is going on and then it puts all of the information together.

The neural network is going to make its way through each layer, checking to see if there is a pattern present inside the image. And if there is a pattern, the neural network is going to activate the process so that it can take a look at the next layer. This process will continue on through this, making its way through the layers as the algorithm is created. Over time, with these predictions and looking through each layer, it will be able to make a good prediction about what is inside that image.

Now, there are a few things that can happen when you end up getting to this point of the process. If the algorithm went through these layers, and then they were able to use that information and makes an accurate prediction there, these neurons are going to start becoming stronger, just like we can see in the brain. This is going to result in a good association between the patterns and the object and the system will soon become more efficient at doing this the next time you decide to use the program.

This can sometimes seem really complicated to work with, so we are going to take a bit of time here to learn more about how these work together and why they can be so effective with machine learning. Let's say that you would like to work on a new kind of program that is able to take the input of a picture, and then recognize that inside the picture, there is a car. The neural networks are going to be able to do this using the features that they know are in a car, including the color, the license plate, and other features.

When you are working with some of the coding methods that you can use with conventional coding methods, you will find that this is a really difficult process to do. But when you add in the neural network system can make this something that is easier to work with.

To get this kind of algorithm to work, you have to make sure that the system at least has the image of a car so it knows what to compare with. The neural network would be able to take a look at that picture of a car. It would start with the first layer, which is going to be the outside edges of the car. Then, as the neural network moves on, it is going to complete different layers of this to help the program learn the unique characteristics that are present inside that picture so that it knows what a car looks like.

Now, if you find that the program is coded the right way and it can do its job, it is going to do a really good job at finding some of the smaller details of the car. This could include some of the things like the windows, the patterns of the wheels, and so much more.

There isn't really a limitation when it comes to how many layers are able to be present in this method. The neural network is going to try and look through as many details and layers as possible. The more that the neural network is able to go through, the more accurate it would be able to predict whether there is a car, and even what type of car it is.

If the neural network is able to accurately identify the model of the car, it is able to learn from this kind of lesson. The program is going to remember the patterns that it found in the picture, and it is going to store them for use if they come across this kind of picture later. Then, the next time that the program is able to encounter this car model, it will make a prediction about the type of car pretty quickly.

This is a good algorithm is one that is often going to be used when you would like to sort through some of the pictures that you have and learn how to sort out the different features that define it. It can be used to help with software that helps with face recognition, for example and can be helpful if you won't be able to put in all of the information ahead of time. Some of the other things that you will be able to do with this will include - recognizing the different types of animals, defining the models of cars, and more.

One of the biggest advantages that you are going to notice when you start to work with neural networks is that there won't be a lot of wasted work in statistical training for this algorithm to work for you. Even without using the statistics in this, you are able to find some of the complex relationships that are going to be present between the two variables, the independent and the dependent variables, even if the two of these don't end up being linear.

Of course, there are sometimes a few drawbacks that you need to be careful about when you are working with this kind of machine learning algorithm. The biggest problem that you need to be careful with is that the neural networks are going to come with costs of computation that are really high. This makes it hard to work with sometimes. For some companies that are high-tech and need to go through a lot of information, this can be worth it. But for other companies, this may cost too much.

Support vector machines

We also need to take a look at the idea of support vector machine learning algorithms. These can also be known as SVM. The SBM is going to be used to help out with many of the challenges that you face in regression and in classification, no matter what your program is trying to work on. With this one, much of the work that you try to do on these problems, especially with classification, can make the work a bit harder to do, but the algorithm is able to help with that as well.

When it is time to work with the algorithm of SVM, you need to be able to take each of the items that are in the set of data, and then plot them together in one point, using the n-dimensional space. N is going to be the number of features that you decide to use for this. Then you will look to the value of all features and how it translates to the value that you find on your chosen coordinate. When you do this, your job has to be determining the hyperplane since this is the part that will help you see the differences between the two classes you are working wit.

There are also going to be a few vectors of support inside of this algorithm that you need to take note of, but you will also notice that these will simply end up being the coordinates of the individual observations that you end up having. You will then be able to use the SVM to be the frontier that helps you separate out all of the classes. With this method, you will end up having two classes when you are all done with the hyperplane and the line.

When you reach this point, you may start to wonder what all of this really means. It seems a bit complicated and you may wonder when and why you would want to use this SVM. Taking a look at some of the ways that you would use this can make it so much easier to use this type of machine learning as well.

The first part of this that we need to take a look at is known as the hyperplane. There are often going to be a few different types of hyperplanes with your data, and you will need to look them over and pick out which one to use. This means that you want to have a method in place to help you pick out the right one ahead of time, the one that is going to work the best for your specific needs.

This is one of the biggest issues and challenges that you need to focus on when you work with the SVM algorithm in machine learning. You want to make sure you aren't wasting your time and even money with the wrong method or the wrong hyperplane, but there are often two or more that you can choose from. The good news here is that there is actually a process that you can choose from to help you take care of this and increases the likelihood that you will be able to pick out the right one. The steps that you can follow to help you pick out and work with the right hyperplane includes

- We are going to start out with three hyperplanes that we will call 1, 2, and 3. Then we are going to spend time figuring out which hyperplane is right so that we can classify the star and the circle.
- The good news is there is a pretty simple rule that you can follow so that it becomes easier to identify which hyperplane is the right one. The hyperplane that you want to go with will be the one that segregates your classes the best.
- That one was easy to work with, but in the next one, our hyperplanes of 1, 2, and 3 are all going through the classes, and they segregate them in a manner that is similar. For example, all of the lines or these

hyperplanes are going to run parallel with each other. From here, you may find that it is hard to pick which hyperplane is the right one.

- For the issue that is above, we will need to use what is known as the margin. This is basically the distance that occurs between the hyperplane and the nearest data point from either of the two classes. Then you will be able to get some numbers that can help you out. These numbers may be closer together, but they will point out which hyperplane is going to be the best.

You will find that the example above is not the only time that you will be able to work with SVM to help with this type of machine learning. When you are taking a look at the data points that you have and you see that there is a clear margin of separation, then the SVM method is most likely the best one to use to help you out. In addition, the effectiveness that you get out of this model will increase any time that you have a project with dimensional spaces that are pretty high. Working on this particular technique can help you to use a subset of training points that come with a decision function, or the support vector, and when the memory of the program you are working on is high enough to allow you to do this.

While there are benefits that you will get with this method depending on the project that you are working on, there are still going to be some times when the SVM method is not the best for you. When you work with a data set that is large, the SVM may not provide you with options that are the most accurate. The training time with these larger sets of data can be high, and this will disappoint you if you need to get through the information quickly. And if there are some target classes that are overlapping, the SVM is going to behave in a way that is different than what you want.

These are a few of the options that you can choose to work with when it comes to working in machine learning that is considered unsupervised. These are a bit easier to work with, but will ensure that you are able to get the program to work the way that you would like it to, without having to go through it all and show every example of what works and what doesn't.

Chapter 7: Reinforcement Machine Learning

Now that we have spent some time talking about supervised and unsupervised learning, it is time to take a look at the third type of machine learning that you are able to work with on your projects. This is one that is known as reinforcement learning, and it will make it easier for you to do a few more things in your projects that won't be done through the algorithms that we have already gone through. If the other two options are not going to work that well for your needs, then it is time to bring out reinforcement machine learning.

If you haven't been able to work with machine learning at all in the past, then you may think that unsupervised learning and reinforcement learning are the same things. And it is true that they are going to share a lot of similarities, but it is important to understand that these are two different types of machine learning.

The first thing to notice is that the input that is given to these algorithms will need to have some mechanism in place to help with feedback. If these are not put in place, then reinforcement learning is not going to work that well for you. You are able to go through and set these up the way that you want. Sometimes they will be positive, and sometimes they will be negative based on which kind of algorithm you would like to get started with.

So, when you decide to start bringing out reinforcement machine learning, you are working with an option that is like trial and error. When you can add in some of the trial and error, you may understand how well this type of learning is going to work. Think about when you are doing some work with a child. When they go through and perform an action that you are not going to approve, you will tell them to stop. Or you may have some other consequence that you use when they don't follow the directions that you want to let them know.

But, things go the other way as well. If your child does something that you approve of, something that you see as good for them, then you will make sure to give them a lot of positive reinforcement, and you will take some time to praise your child. When you do this, the positive reinforcement when they are good and the consequence when they are doing something you don't approve of, can help your child to really learn what they are able to do and what they can't.

To make this as simple as possible, the trial and error option from above is going to be similar to what you will find with reinforcement machine learning. It works on the idea that trial and error is the best way for a program to learn what it should do for each situation and input that the user decides to work with. A reinforcement algorithm is going to be used in order to help your chosen program make decisions.

You will find that this kind of learning is a great one to work with any time that you would like to bring in an algorithm that is able to make decisions without any mistakes and will come up with the best outcome each time. Of course, make sure that you understand that when you do this one, it can take some time for the program to get accurate results because it needs to learn what you want it to do. You can add this learning to the code that you write, ensuring that the computer is able to learn the way that you want it to.

Now that we know a bit more about reinforcement learning and what it all entails, we need to take a look at some of the different algorithms that you are able to use when you want to learn this way. Some of the most common reinforcement machine learning algorithms that you are able to work with include:

Q-learning

There are going to be a variety of algorithms that you can work with when you need to bring in reinforcement learning that you can work with, and the first of these options that you may want to work with is called Q-learning. This algorithm is going to work the best if you would like to work with the temporal difference learning. As you are trying to work with some of the different algorithms here, you will probably notice that this one is kind of like an algorithm that is off-policy because it has the ability to learn an action value function, which means that no matter what kind of state you would be in, you will get the results that you were expecting.

Since you can use this particular algorithm for any function that you want, you must go through and list out the specifications for how the user or the learner will select the course of action.

After you, the programmer, go through and then find the action value function that you want to use, then it is time to work on the optimal policy. You can work on constructing this by using the actions that will have the highest value no matter what state you are working with.

A big advantage of working with Q-learning is that you won't need to provide it with models of the environment for you to compare the utility of all your actions. What this means is that you are able to compare a few or many, actions together, and you will not need to worry about the type of environment that you are going to use with it.

SARSA

The other algorithm that you are able to work with when you are looking at a reinforcement machine learning algorithm is known as the SARSA algorithm or the state action reward state action algorithm. For this kind of option, you are going to need to learn how to take the time to describe the decision process policy that will occur with that Markov algorithm that we talked about in an earlier chapter.

This would then be the main function that you would use with the updated -value which will then rely on whatever the current state of the learner is. It can also include the reward that the learner is going to get for the selection they make, the action that the learner chooses, and then the new state that the learner is going to be in when they are done with that action. As you can see, there are a ton of different parts that will end up coming together in order to make the SARSA work for your needs.

While there are many parts that must come together for this one, this is sometimes seen as the safest algorithm for a programmer to use when they are trying to find the solution they want to use. However, there can possibly be times when your learner is going to end up with a reward that is higher than what the average is for their trials. This is a bigger issue with the SARSA compared to some of the other algorithms that you have.

There are also going to be times when the learner ends up not going with the optimal path either. Depending on how the program decides to react to this, it could bring up some issues with how they learn and how the program is going to behave for them.

There are some times when the reinforcement learning that you do is going to look pretty similar to what you can find with unsupervised machine learning. However, this option is going to spend time working on trial and error for how it solves problems instead. This can actually end up opening up a lot of opportunities that you may not be able to do when you work with a supervised or an unsupervised machine learning algorithms that we talked about earlier in this guidebook.

These are the basic types of reinforcement machine learning options that you are able to work with in order to make it easier to get the program to work the way that you would like. Take some time to work with each of these, and learn better how they are going to react to your program the way that it should behave overall.

Chapter 8: Top Applications of Working with Machine Learning

We have spent quite a bit of time learning about what all machine learning is about, and how amazing it can be for some of the programming that you want to be able to work with. There are so many different things and applications that are going to use this type of coding, and as technology starts to become more advanced and changes in the future, it is likely that more and more applications are going to be developed at the same time as well.

There are already a lot of applications that are going to be used on a regular basis, along with machine learning. Some of the most common ones are going to include options like image recognition, speech recognition, and predictions for many major companies when they are trying to sort through their data and know which way they should take their business in the future. With that in mind, let's explore a bit more about some of the top applications that you will be able to use with machine learning.

Image recognition

One of the most common applications of machine learning is that of image recognition. Most phones and many laptops are going to be able to use this kind of algorithm to help them recognize the faces of the users who are on them. There are a lot of different situations where you may want the technology that you have to be able to classify a certain object and tell you what is in the image. The measurements of each digital image that you want to pull up are going to give the user an idea of the output of each pixel in the image.

So, let's say that you want to look at an image that is all in black and white, the intensity that comes with all f the pixels that are in that image would help because they serve as the measurement. If the image ends up having M*M pixels, then we would denote this as having a measurement of M^2.

The cool thing is that when the machine has this kind of software put on it, it can go into the picture and split up the pixels so that you end up having three different measurements. These help you to know what the intensity level of the three primary colors, namely RBG, are. So, with the idea of M*M from before, then there are going to be three M^2 measurements.

Another part that comes with this is face detection. This is one of the most common categories that comes with image recognition software, and it is used in order to help detect whether the image has a face or not. There can also be a different category that is added in that allows you to make a new category for each person in your database.

You can also work with a part that is known as character recognition. When you add this to your machine learning program, you are able to segment out each piece of writing into the images of small sizes where each image contain one character. These categories are going to be comprised of the 26 letters of the English alphabet, as well as the first ten numbers and any special characters that come with it.

As you can see, there are already a lot of cool things that you are able to do when it comes to image recognition. It can help you to do security issues, recognition on some social media sites as well. Being able to recognize what is inside an image and developing more and more technology to help with this is definitely something that we should expect in the future.

Speech recognition

Another thing that machine learning is able to help out with is the process of speech recognition. This is when an application is able to take spoken words, and either translates it back into some actual text or when it is able to follow a command of what you are telling it to do, including what we see with Amazon Echo and other similar products. Experts are going to refer to this kind of application in a few different ways, including Computer Speech Recognition, Speech to Text, and Automatic Speech Recognition.

The programmer is able to use this in order to take spoken words and then trains the machine in order to recognize speech and to convert the words into text. Google and Facebook are two mainstream programs that are going to use this kind of method to help train their machines. This works because the machines are going to use measurements in order to represent the signal of speech. These signals are going to then be further split up into distinct phenomes and words. The algorithm, if it is set up the right way, is going to use different kinds of energies in order to represent the signals that the speech sends out.

The details that you are able to see with this representation are going to be a bit more than what we will talk about in this book, but it is important to know that all of the signals are going to relate back to real signals. Applications that are out there that help with speech recognition will also be able to include an interface for the voice user, some of these including things like voice dialing and call routing on your phone. Depending on the application, these are able to use data entry and some of the other simple methods that are used to process information.

Prediction

Let's take some time to use our imagination here in order to think about how a bank works. In this scenario, a bank is going to try and calculate the probability of whether an applicant for a loan is going actually to pay for their loans or default on repayment. To help them to calculate this kind of probability of risk, the system needs first to be able to identify, clean, and classify the data that is available in groups.

The analysts are going to classify the data based on certain criteria. Prediction is one of the most sought after uses of machine learning. And there are so many ways that it is able to be used. First, you will find many companies want to be able to use this in a way to help them to figure out whether or not they should take one action or another in order to help them to grow. This can help a bank figure out if one of their applicants is going to keep paying the loan. It can help retailers to figure out the best way to advertise their products to their customers, and it can help to figure out how sales will do in the future.

Anyone who has to do forecasts and make guesses about the way that their business should go in the future is going to be able to benefit from this kind of technology. Instead of having to sift through all of the information on their own and hoping they get it right, or being new to the business and not having enough experience to back up the decisions, these business owners and decision makers are able to go in and use some of the algorithms of machine learning.

Machine learning, including a few of the algorithms that we talked about in this guidebook, are going to be able to take a look at all of the information and data that you have. this could include information on customers, on their buying habits, on inventory, and past sales to name a few. It will then compute the information, and show the likely outcome, based on past events, that something is going to work for you or not. This makes it easier to know which decisions need to be made for your business.

Of course, these are not going to be accurate all of the time. There are going to be times when the predictions are going to be wrong, such as if there is a big change in the industry or the economy ends up going down. But they are going to be more accurate than what most humans can do on their own. And having someone who watches the market and prepares in case something drastic does change, and doing these predictions on a regular basis will make a big difference.

Medical diagnosis

Machine learning is going to provide us with a number of methods, tools, and techniques that a doctor is able to use in their field to salve any diagnostic and prognostic problems at work. Doctors and patients can both use these techniques in order to enhance their medical knowledge and analyze the symptoms in order to figure out what the prognosis.

The results that you are able to get from this kind of analysis can be very valuable. You will find that it is able to really open up the medical knowledge that most doctors have. Even skilled professionals are going to find there are certain conditions and treatments that they don't know about, and being able to work with machine learning can help them to do their job more efficiently. Doctors are able to use this machine learning in order to identify the irregularities in unstructured data, the interpretation of continuous data and to monitor results efficiently.

The use of this and how successful it is will help it to integrate computer-based systems with the healthcare environment and because this helps those in the medical world with a lot of opportunities to enhance and even improve the types of treatments that they can provide.

When we are looking at a medical diagnosis, the interest that comes with this is to establish the existence of the disease that is there, and then the doctor needs to work in order to identify the disease accurately. There are different categories for each disease that are under consideration, and then they can add in a category for a different disease that may not be present. Then, with the help of machine learning, it helps to improve the accuracy of a diagnosis and analyzes the data of the patients. The measurements used are the results of the many medical tests conducted on the patient. The doctors are going to identify the disease using these measurements.

Statistical arbitrage

The next thing that you are going to be able to use machine learning is known as statistical arbitrage. This is a term that is going to be used in finance, so if you are working in this kind of field, it is going to be a good one to focus on. This will refer to the science of using trading strategies to help identify some of the securities that are short term which one can invest in.

When using these kinds of strategies, the user is able to implement in an algorithm on an array of securities based on the general economic variables and the historical correlation of the data. The type of measurement that you are going to be able to use will help to resolve any problems that you have with estimation and classification. The assumption is that the stock price is going to always stay near its historical average overall.

Another strategy to focus on is the index arbitrage. This is going to be a strategy that is going to rely on the methods we have discussed with machine learning. The linear regression, as well as the support vector regression algorithms that we talked about before, are going to be so useful in helping the user calculate out the different prices that you will see with the funds and the stocks that you are interested in. and if you add in the principal component analysis, you will see that the algorithm breaks the data into various dimensions, which are used to identify the trading signals as a mean reverting process.

When it comes to investing, there are a lot of different parts that come into play, and being able to keep them organized and knowing how to use them with machine learning can take some practice. The buy, hold, sold, put, call or do nothing are just a few of the categories under which the algorithm places these securities under, based on what you want to do with it overall. The algorithm is then going to get to work helping you to calculate out the returns that you should expect in the future on each security. These estimates are going to help the user decide which security they want to buy and which security they would like to sell.

Learning associations

The final application that we are going to focus on when it comes to machine learning is known as the learning association. This is basically the process of trying to develop a good insight into the association between different groups of products that you have. There will be several products that are responsible for revealing this association, even if the two products or variables seem like they are completely unrelated. This kind of algorithm is useful because it takes into account the buying habits of the customers in order to figure out the best associations that are present.

One of these types of learning associations that can be used is known as basket learning analysis. This one, in particular, is going to deal with studying the association between products that were purchased by different customers. It is a type of application that works well at showing us how machine learning works.

With this one, we will assume that our Customer A bought product X. based on this purchase, we are going to use the options from machine learning in order to identify whether she is going to purchase product Y based on how these two products are associated together.

To make this easier, we can use the example of fish and chips to get the concept to work. If you have a new product that comes into the market, the association that was there between the previously existing products will also change. Sometimes it will change quite a bit, and sometimes the products are not related much to the new one, and their association is not going to change all that much. If one already knows the relationships between various products, they are able to go through and identify the right product to recommend to their customers.

And this is also one of the reasons that a lot of companies are happy to introduce their products in pairs, rather than individually. This helps them to promote two products, and make a bigger sale, by predicting the needs that their customer will have ahead of time and then meeting the need. If the customer sees two related products that go together and they are released at the same time, they are more likely to purchase both of these products together, knowing that they go together, and it increases the purchasing power and the capital for the company.

Big Data analysts are going to work with machine learning on a regular basis in order to help them figure out what relationship is there when it comes to different products from the same company. The algorithms are going to be there and can often use the idea of probability and statistics, like we talked about earlier in this guidebook, to help come up with the relationship that is present in these products, and to help the company figure out which other products the customer is likely to purchase after they purchase the first one.

As you can see here, there are a number of different ways that machine learning is able to be used. And it can be used across a wide variety of different industries and in many ways. Whether it comes to using it to recommend products for a customer, you use it to make some predictions, or for some other reason, you will find that the things that machine learning is able to do already, and the applications that it is likely to be able to do in the future are already pretty amazing.

Chapter 9: Other Algorithms to Use in Machine Learning

In this guidebook, we have already talked about quite a few of the algorithms that you are able to use when it comes to working with machine learning. There are a lot of different ones that are available to make life a bit easier as well, but now, we are going to cover a few more of the ones that you may find useful if you are trying to progress some of your skills a bit more. Some of the other machine learning algorithms that you are able to use in order to help train any machine that you are using includes:

Dimension Reduction Methods

When we take a look at some of the databases that you may be using, it is possible that there could be millions or more records and variables that are there. And you will need to use all of these variables in order to derive a good training data set. It is impossible to conclude that the variables are not going to be dependent on one another with any kind of correlation between them. It is important for you to remember that there are often going to be more than one similarity between the variables. In this kind of situation, the predictor variable is going to be correlated in some way, and this is often going to have some kind of effect on the output.

Now, there are going to be times when there is a lot of instability arises in the solution set when there is multicollinearity between the variables leading to incoherent results. For example, with this, if you are trying to look at more than one regression, there are multiple correlations between the predictor variables that have a significant impact on the output set.

However, individual predictor variables may not have a significant impact on the solution set. But, you may find that even when the programmer is able to identify a way to remove this kind of instability (and they will often strive to make that happen), then there are still going to be times when their user, or the one who is going to use the program at some point, may include variables with a high level of correlation between them. When this does happen, the algorithm will need to focus more on some parts of the input vector more than to the others.

Now, you may have a data set that ends up with more than one kind of predictor variable, and when this happens, there is going to be a new complication that shows up. This complication is going to be where the algorithm must identify a model between the predictor and the variables that end up responding. This situation is going to complicate the analysis and its interpretation and violates the principle of parsimony.

So, what is this principle all about? This principle is going to state that as an analyst who is using machine learning, should always stick to a certain number of predictor variables, which makes it easy for human beings, as well as machines, in order to interpret the results. It is tempting to go through and retain a lot of different variables. But when this happens, there is going to be some possibility of a problem known as overfitting. You can try to do this, but it is likely that it is going to hinder the analysis that you are able to get in the long run. Picking out one predictor to work with and getting everything else to fit with it is going to be the best.

The goal of working with this kind of method in machine learning is that we want to use the structure of correlation among the different variables of prediction. The reason that this is going to be done in this method is to help the programmer work towards the following goals:

1. Reduce the number of components for prediction in the set of data that you are using.
2. It can ensure that the components that you are using for predictions are going to still be independent of one another.

3. It can predict you with a framework that is dynamic, which is going to help in interpreting this kind of analysis.

There are a few methods that go under the idea of dimension reduction and those are known as User Defined Composites and Factor Analysis and Principal Component Analysis.

Clustering

Another method that we need to take some time to explore here is known as clustering. This is going to be a technique of machine learning that is able to group different data points into a set of data that is similar. A programmer is often going to use this type of algorithm because it is able to take all of the points of data that they are using and will group them together into groups that fit them the best.

The variables or the points of data that end up going into the same group need to be able to bear some similarities to one another. But the variables that are found in different groups shouldn't be alike at all. This needs to happen as much as possible. Clustering is known as one of the unsupervised machine learning algorithms and it is often used when it is time to work with an analysis of a lot of statistical data.

Data scientists often like to use this kind of analysis of clustering in order to get some better insights into all of the data they have. if you have millions of points of data, it is hard to compute them all and understand what each one means and how it is going to be able to influence what you know and what you do with your points. But when you work with clustering, all of the information is going to be put into different groups (The number of groups will depend on how much data you have and how you can divide it up), and it will help you to read the information better than before.

There are going to be a few different types of clustering that you are able to work with depending on the kind of information that you need to cluster, how many categories you would like it split into, and more. Let's take a look at a few of these and see what they are all about and when you would use them.

K-Means

The K-Means clustering algorithm is one of the first ones that we are going to take a look at here. This one comes with the concept that every data scientist and engineer and anyone else who uses machine learning needs to know how to use it to get the right results. This is one that you really should learn more about because it is easy to add into your code and will ensure you are able to get the results that you would like. Some of the things that you will notice when it comes to the K-means algorithm   include:

1. The algorithm is going to start out the process by selecting the number of classes and the groups that you want to use. You will also need to come up with an

idea of where the center points of these groups will be. If you are starting out with a lot of data and you are not sure how many classes should be used, you can look through the data and see if you can get some ideas. You can also mess around with this a bit and experiment until you find the right number that seems to work for you.

2. The algorithm is then going to get to work trying to classify what the points of data are. It is able to do this by calculating the distance between the point and all of your center points. The programmer is then able to take a look at this distance and use it in order to categorize the data point in the class whose center is the closest to that point.

3. Using these classified points that you just figured out, the algorithm is then going to be able to compute where the center of the points is in the class, by utilizing the mean here.

4. The programmer then needs to go through these steps a few times. It is going to continue doing this until the

center of the groups does not change between the different iterations that you decide to do. You can also go through and try to initialize the centers in the groups at random, and then select an iteration that is going to give you the best results overall.

This is a clustering algorithm that you may need to use on a regular basis. It has the advantage that it is so simple and fast to use, so it makes it really easy to use as a beginner since you are going to be able to use it in a way to compute the distance between the variables and the center of the group. This works well because it gives you a good way to organize the information that you have.

Of course, there are going to be a few disadvantages that are going to come with this option. First, you need to be able to accurately select the number of classes that you want to add into this simply by looking at the data. And if you have a ton of data, you may find that this is not ideal. And since you may want to find some insight about the data that you are using, it isn't ideal either. And since there are going to be some times when you will need to be random in how you select the center points that you use in the groups, this may cause you to come up with different results for each iteration.

If you want a method that is simple and easy to use and can help to separate out your data points pretty well, then this method is going to be a great one that you should try out. With that said, there are going to be some times when you are not going to like working with this. You have to look at your data and figure out whether or not this is the right option for you.

Mean shift clustering

Another type of clustering that you may choose to work with is known as the mean shift clustering. This is going to be something that a programmer is able to use when they want to figure out and look through the dense areas that show up in their set of data. This algorithm is also useful because it will take a look at the center points of every group.

However, the main goal that you are going to see with this kind of algorithm is that it is able to do some updates to some of the possible center points of the class within the sliding windows to locate the center point that you want. This can make it a bit better than the K-Means that we talked about before.

This mean shift clustering algorithm is going to remove the points that it chose for the center after it has gotten to the processing stage because this helps it to reduce some of the duplicates that can sometimes form with these. And once it does this, the algorithm is going to move on to forming the final set of cluster points and placing them in their groups.

Let us first take a look at how this is going to look. Let us consider a set of points in a two-dimensional space. The first step that we need to take here is to define the point around which the circular sliding window is positioned. This window is going to have a radius of r called the kernel. This algorithm is going to be a hill-climbing algorithm and it is constantly going to move the kernel to denser regions until the values are able to converge and come together.

Going back to this sliding window, it is going to continue to move to a denser region at every iteration. The algorithm is able to do this by shifting the center point of all the groups until you get the point that shows up at the mean. The density of the points in this window is going to be proportional to the number of data points that are found inside of it. So, if there are more points in this, this means that the density is going to be higher as well.

What this all means for you is that when you see a shift in the algorithm, it means that the mean of the point in the window is going to start moving over to the areas where the data seems to be denser than the other places.

This sliding window is going to keep on moving according to the change that shows up in the mean. The direction is not going to matter. It just depends on where the mean ends up in all of this. The algorithm will then continue going through all of these steps, working with sliding windows that always change, until it is able to categorize all f the points of data that are found in the set into different sliding windows.

If you do decide to use this method, you will not have to select the number of clusters or classes, which is one of the best advantages that come with this. It is also good that the center points are going to converge together using a mean, and it moves to the mean that is found in the area that is the densest out of all of them. This is because this kind of algorithm is going to really understand the data, and it will try to fit it into any application that is driven by data. The selection of the kernel is not going to be as important with this one, but that, in some cases, is a major drawback that starts to occur.

If you are a beginner with the whole idea of machine learning and the clustering algorithms, then working with the K-means algorithm is going to be the best bet. But once you have a good understanding of how this method works and whether you will be able to use it for your needs or not, you will be able to try out the other algorithms for clustering to help make your analysis a bit better.

Working with regression modeling

Now that we have taken some time to explore what the world of clustering is all about in machine learning, it is time to move it a bit further and talk about regression modeling. This is an algorithm that is going to be used if the programmer would like to be able to estimate the values of continuous target variables. There are going to be a variety of regression models that you are able to choose from.. but one of the simplest forms of this that you can use is going to be the linear regression model.

With the linear regression model, the algorithm is going to try and define the relationship that happens between a continuous predictor variable and a continuous response variable using a straight line. there are going to be models that can use more than one of these variables for predicting things in order to define the response the variable.

Apart from the models that we already mentioned, there are going to be two other algorithms that can fit with this. These are called the logistic regression methods and the least squared regression. However, there are going to be some assumptions that come with these models can create some disparities. It is important that if you use this one a bit, you are going to need to validate the assumptions that you have there before you write out the algorithm and before you even think about building the model.

If you have an engineer that will build up a model and they use it without verifying the assumptions, then you have to be aware of the fact that you will get an output and you won't be able to use it since the model may have failed without the knowledge of the engineer.

When the programmer does get the result, they need to go through and check that there isn't going to be a linear relationship that shows up between the different variables of the models. There are going to be times when the set of data is going to have some variables that may be hidden with the linear relationship that they have. however, there is going to be a systematic approach that is there, known as inference, which the programmer can use in order to determine the kind of linear relationship that is there.

We need to take a look at some of the inference methods that the programmer is able to use in order to determine the kind of relationship that is there. Some of the best inference methods that you are able to use includes:

1. The t-test. This is going to be used in order to help you know the relationship between your two variables, the predictor and the response.
2. The confidence interval for the slope that shows up.
3. The confidence interval for the mean of the response variable given a value of the predictor.

4. The interval for the prediction that works for your random value of the response variable, given a value of the predictor.

The methods that are described above are going to often depend on the assumption that the programmer decides to make at the beginning of the process. It is easy for the programmer to assess whether the data is able to stick with the assumptions that you come with. You are able to check your assumptions with two main graphical methods. You will be able to do a plot of the standardized residuals and the plot of the normal probability.

A normal probability plot is going to be a quantile to quantile plot of the quantiles of distribution against the quantiles of a standard normal distribution for the purposes of determining whether the distribution is going to deviate from what is seen as the normal or the mean. When you work with this kind of plot, the programmer is going to be able to make some comparisons between the value that they observe for the distribution of interest, and compare it to the expected number of values that seem to occur with a distribution that is seen as normal.

If the programmer goes through and does this one, the bulk of the points in the plot should end up falling on or near a straight line. if there is a deviation from this kind of plot, it is going to be seen as a deviation. A programmer is then able to validate their assumptions for the regression by seeing what patterns are going to show up on their plat. If they do notice a pattern is showing up, then the programmer is able to identify which assumptions don't seem to hold true that well. However, if there isn't a pattern that shows up, then the assumptions can stay intact.

If you are taking a look through the graphs and they indicate that there is some violation of the assumptions you made, you may be able to apply a transformation to the response variable y, such as the ln (natural log or the log to the base of e) transformation. If the relationship between the response variables and the variables used for prediction, then the algorithm can be used for transformation.

Gaussian Mixture Models

The next thing that we are going to talk about is known as the Gaussian mixture models. These are a form of density estimation that you are able to use, and they will help to give you an approximation of the probability distribution of your data. You are going to chose this kind of model when you notice that the data you are using is multi-modal. This means that there are going to be more than one bump or mode in the histogram. If you remember what we talked about with probability, the mode is simply the values that are the most common.

So the Gaussian mixture will basically be the sum of the weighted Gaussians. To represent these weights, we're going to introduce a brand new symbol that we need to be called pi. We are going to say pi(k) is the probability that your x value is going to belong to the kth Gaussian. Since pi(k) is a probability, there is going to be a constraint that all the pi's need to have a sum of 1. If this is confusing, another method that you can think of this is that we introduced a new latent variable that is called "z." "Z" is going to represent which Gaussian the data was coming from. So we can basically say pi(k) = P(z=k).

It is similar to saying that there is some hidden cause that is called "z" that we don't know about and we aren't able to measure from the beginning. But each of the "z"s is causing a new Gaussian to be generated, and we will be able to see that the data we place into the system is going to be the combined effects of those individual "z"s.

Training with the GMM is pretty similar to the k-means algorithm that we used earlier, which will make it a bit easier to learn. There are two main steps that you will be able to use to figure out the Gaussian, and they will be similar to what you use with the k-means.

The first step is to calculate the responsibilities. For this one, r(k,n) is going to be the responsibility of the kth Gaussian for generating the nth point. So it's just the proportion of that Gaussian, and then divide it by all of the Gaussians too. You can see that if pi(k) is larger here, then it is going to be able to overtake the other Gaussians, and it should be about the value of 1. The algorithm that you would use for this one includes:

r(k,n) = pi(k)N(x(n), mu(k), C(k)) / sum[j=1..K]{pi(j)N(x(n), mu(j), C(j)) }

When working with the C(k), this is going to mean the covariance of the kth Gaussian. The N9x, mu, C) means the probability density function) of your Gaussian of the data point x and the mean mu and covariance C.

Once you have done this part, it is time to move on to step number two. This step is to go through and recalculate all of the parameters of your Gaussians. This means the pi's, covariances, and the means. The method for going through and doing this is going to be pretty similar to what we did with the k-means, where we are going to weigh the influence of each sample on the parameter by using the responsibility. If the responsibility of the sample is small, this means that the "x" is going to matter less in the total of the calculation. Let's look at how we would go through and do this.

Define: $N(k)$ as $N(k) = \text{sum}[n=1..N]\{\ r(k,n)\}$

Then each of the parameter updates will be the following:

$\text{mu}(k) = \text{sum}[n=1..N]\{\ r(k,n)x(n)\ ]\ /\ N(k)$

$C(k) = \text{sum}[n=1..N]\{\ r(k,n)(x(n) - \text{mu}(k))(x(n) - \text{mu}(k))\}\ /\ N(k)$

$\text{pi}(k) = N(k)\ /\ N$

These are just a few of the different algorithms that you are able to use when it comes to working with machine learning. As you read through this guidebook, you can start to see there are a lot of different options when it comes to working with machine learning. And often it is going to depend on what use you have for it from the beginning. If you want to be able to look through and sort through all of the data you have, you may use one algorithm but if you want to guess what products your past customers are going to use and purchase in the future, then the algorithm you use is going to be different.

And that is the beauty of working with machine learning. You will find that because there are already so many applications of working with machine learning, and it is likely that it is going to continue growing throughout time, that these numerous learning behaviors are going to be necessary and ore of them will come up in the future. Learning more about this process of how machine learning is able to make a difference in the coding that you are able to use.

174

Conclusion

Thank for making it through to the end of *Machine Learning* let's hope it was informative and able to provide you with all of the tools you need to achieve your goals whatever they may be.

The next step is to get started with some of the building blocks, information, and algorithms that we talked about in this guidebook. There is so much to love when it comes to working with machine learning, and many people are just starting out and have no idea what all of this even means. This guidebook is meant to help you to get started, to gain a better understanding of what machine learning is all about, and even how to start using it in your own business, or on some of your own projects.

This guidebook took some time to discuss more about machine learning and all of the cool things that you are able to do with it. You will enjoy that it can help to sort through large amounts of data (which is useful for any business who wants to plan out for the future in the most efficient manner), works with search engines, voice recognition and so much more. If you can imagine a project that you want to do, but you worry that traditional coding languages are going to struggle with it, then this guidebook and the machine learning techniques that are inside will be the right option for you.

From there, we spent some time bringing it all together and exploring some of the cool things that you are able to do when working with machine learning. We talked about how it compares to artificial intelligence, some of the basic building blocks and some examples that you need to know when you are just getting started, and then we moved on to some of the best algorithms that you can use, based on the situation and the project on hand. When you put all of this information together, you will be able to find plenty of uses for machine learning and how to make it work for you.